Wipf and Stock Publishers
199 W 8th Ave, Suite 3
Eugene, OR 97401

The Constitutional Blues
By Becker, Ted L. and Lantz, Patricia
Copyright©2015 by Becker, Ted L.
ISBN 13: 978-1-5326-3656-1
Publication date 6/30/2017
Previously published by Blurb, 2015

The Constitutional Blues

Originally Published in
The Haiku Blues
Haiku that take you on a journey through pain, love, politics and soul
By Ted Becker and Patricia Lantz

WIPF *&* STOCK · Eugene, Oregon

The Haiku Blues

I write haiku when
I'm feelin' blue and when love and
pain make me want to.

Other Books by the Authors

The Haiku Blues

Deluxe Limited Edition

The Haiku Blues
Trade Edition

Full Spectrum of Blue

The Soul Bendin' Blues

The Divorce Blues

Table of Contents

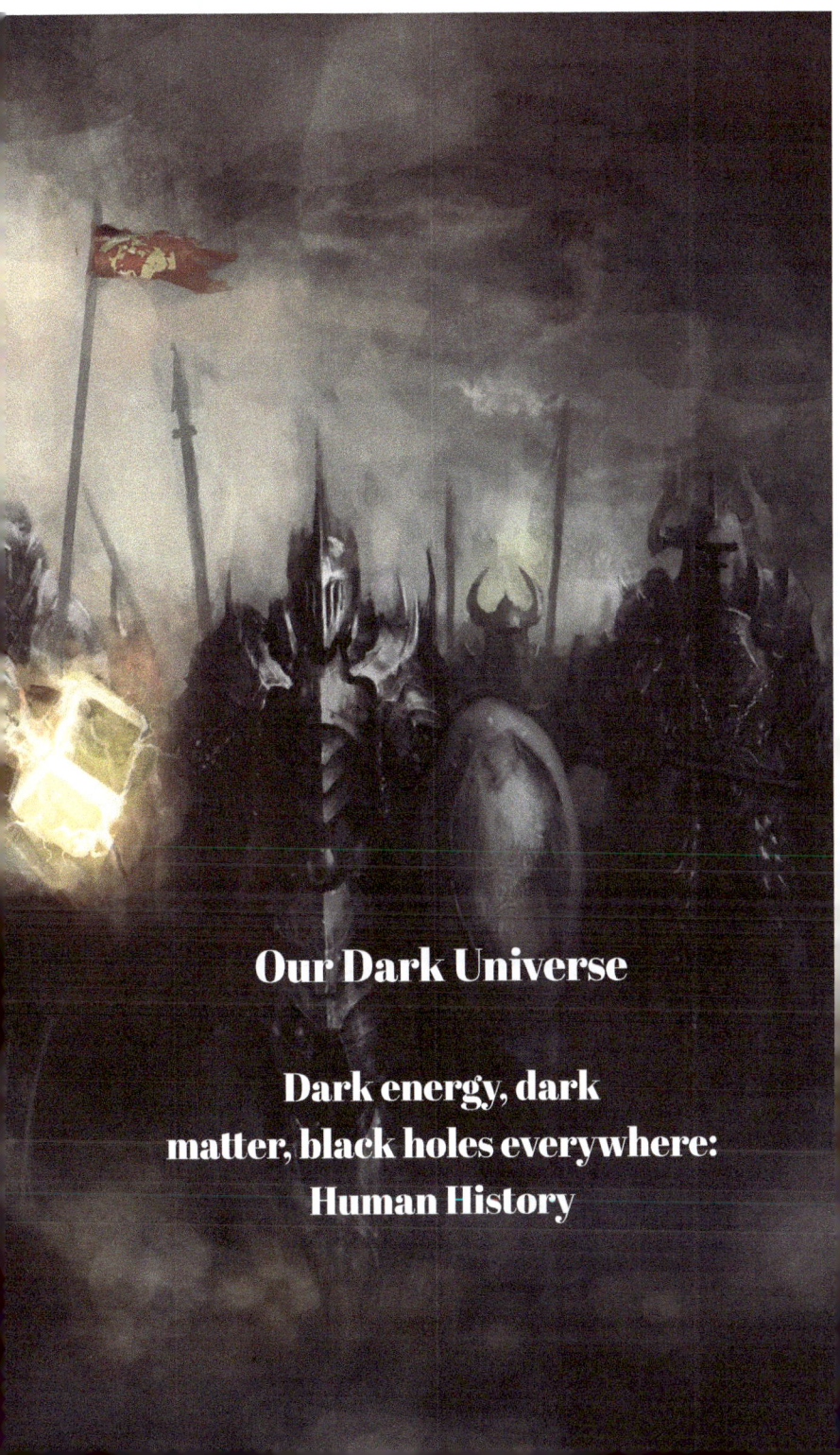

Our Dark Universe

Dark energy, dark matter, black holes everywhere: Human History

The New 4th of July

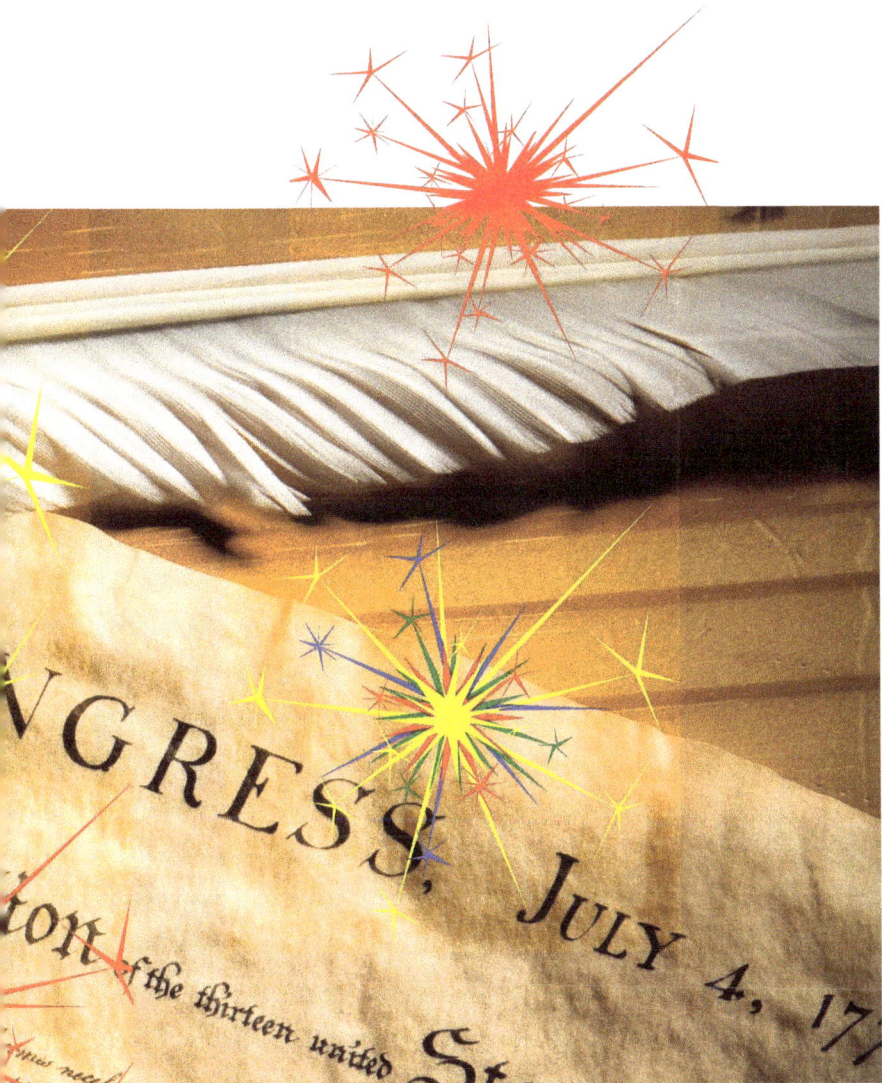

Lustrous words of yore
dimmed by fireworks, silenced by
bluster, now a bore.

Myth America

It's boasting we're just,
"democratic" and lawful
that makes our wars grate.

"Forgotten Founders"

Splattered, scattered and battered, their culture endures, and beckons to us.

California Dreaming

Where our "manifest destiny" shoulda stopped and our future flip flopped.

America's Genius

Luring brains over business lanes-Europe's, Asian and those screwed by Spain.

The American "Free" Press

Grand illusions of ruthless media spinning truthless conclusions.

American Politics: Ala Carte

**Vintage whines, followed
by baloney wrapped in ham.
For dessert: Trifles**

Free Enterprise

**Victims of Laissez-
Faire: isolated, selfish, bare:
Hapless meals for wolves**

The High and (not so) Mighty

High strife, high tech, high
life, prep schooled, low piety,
high anxiety.

The American Legal System

Two-tiered, much feared, too long, incomprehensible, indispensable.

The Late, Unlamented Right to Privacy

Bar codes in the brain, scanners in the sky. Yourself? Repealed by Congress

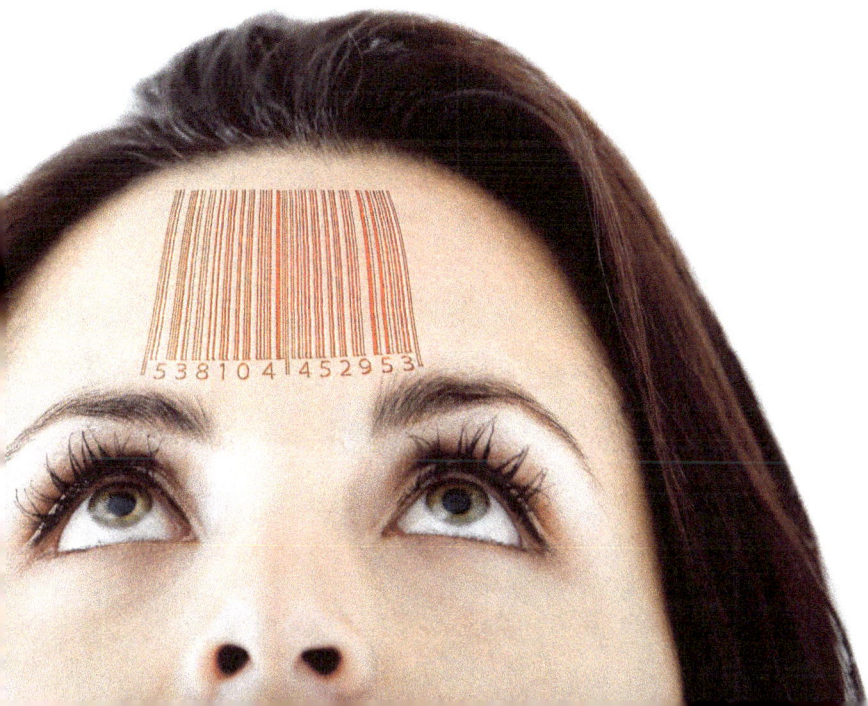

The Childlike World of Geopolitics

Checkers, with lethal
toys, where grand strategy is
in the loins of boys.

Fair Exchange

Canucks go south for
less taxed frills, while Yanks head north
for much cheaper pills.

Help Fight the U.S. Work Force

Stock values equal a rigged Dow, union busting, jobs to Asia. Buy now!

Discount the Truth

Elections are not referenda. They are "sales" of hidden agendas.

The "New" World Order

IMF, World Bank, and NATO, madmen puffed with power. So what's new?

The Bottom Line for Global Corporations

Soil dispoilers, air polluters, tax evaders, traitors to nations.

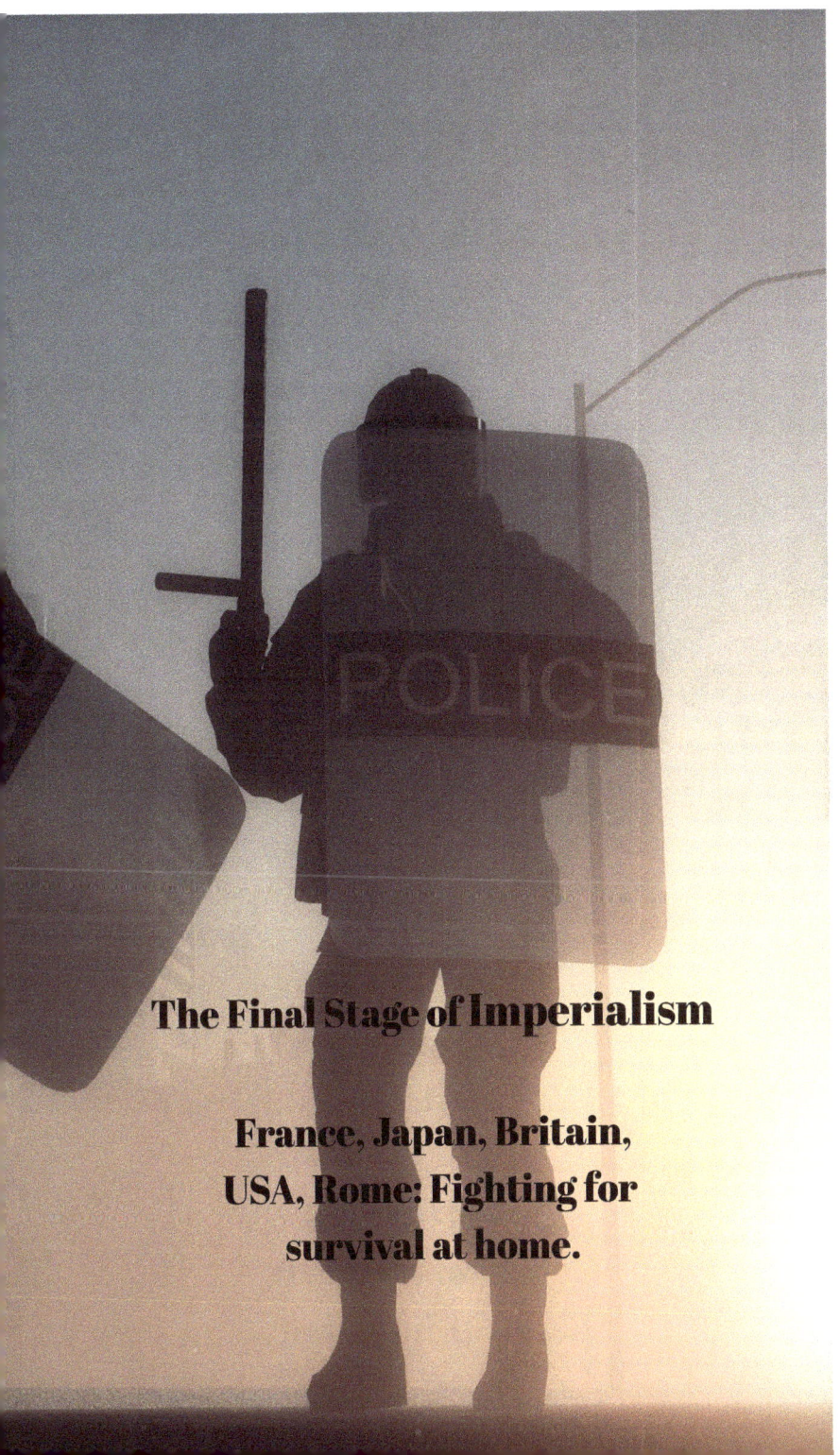

The Final Stage of Imperialism

France, Japan, Britain, USA, Rome: Fighting for survival at home.

The Looming Global Cataclysm

**Catastrophe is
Gaia's immunity: To
cure our infection.**

Wall Street Logic

**Greed, fear, and despair:
the 'rational' motives of
wild-eyed bulls and bears.**

If Only the Public Knew

**Until the people
are involved, global issues
will go unresolved.**

The President as Prisoner

He only knows what
he's told by evil schemers.
Leaders are dreamers.

The Next Constitutional Convention

**When a people know
their system's been choked and nixed,
it needs to be fixed.**

Those who empower
others aren't heretics.
It's their genetics.

The Democracy Gene

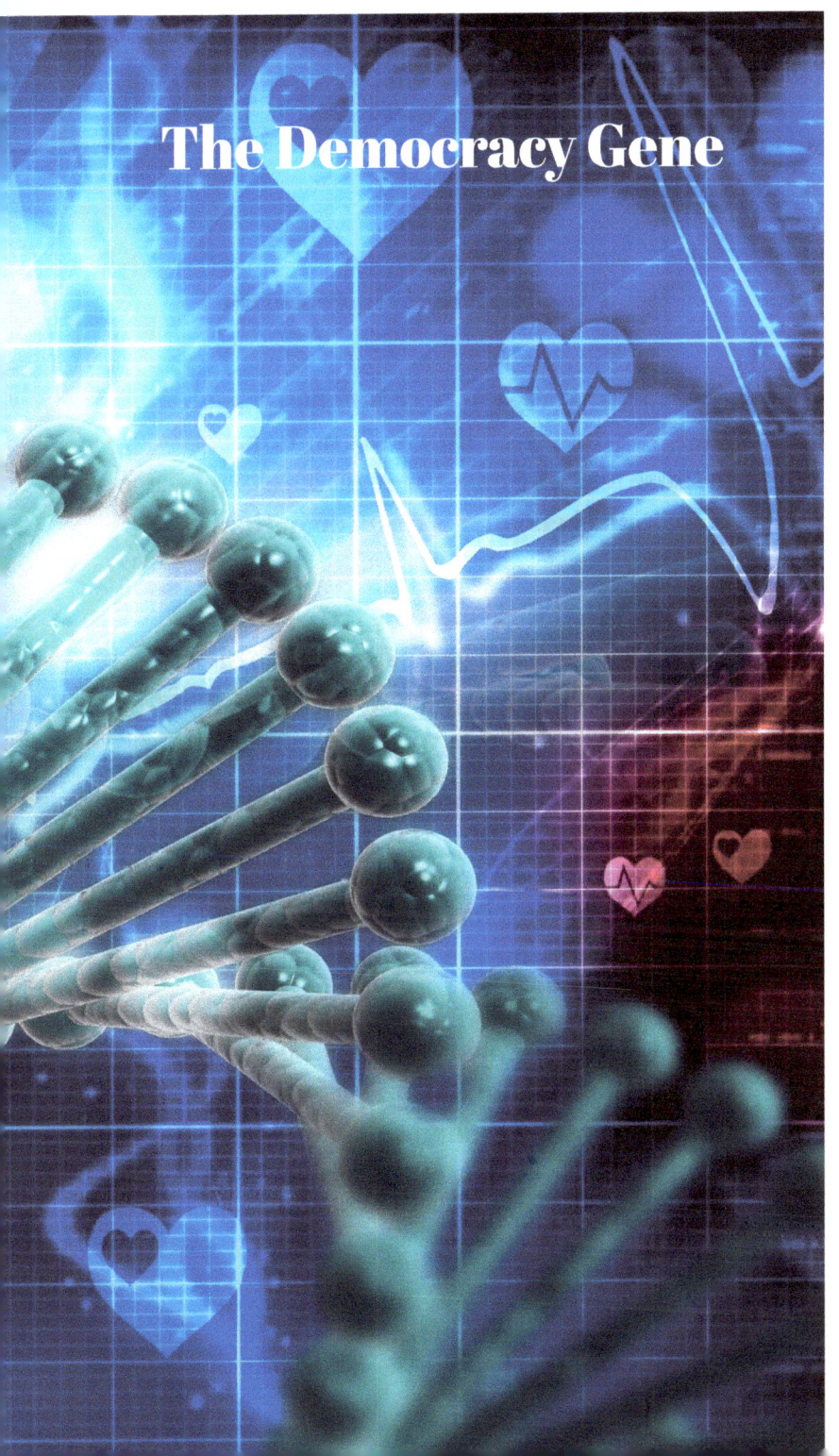

The Wrong Obsessions

Your were sent here for good reason
but given little information.
To those few who pass through, it's a brief season
in their spirit's transformation.

What little play you have in life
you must stoke love's flame from birth.
Despite all you gain from work and strife,
it's the only thing you take from Earth.

For whatever cause, if it gets extinguished,
the consequence is utter devastation.
All that's left for you is latent anguish
over your next reincarnation.

So, if this sad world is where you want to be
then wallow in your possessions.
The next time around you may come to see
You were the author of the wrong obsessions.

The Democracy Amendments

* Citizens Initiative – Citizens Veto – Referendum
(Switzerland, NZ, California, Maine + Many More)

* Repeal Corporate Personhood

* End the Fed
(North Dakota State Bank Model)

* Repeal Electoral College
(Direct Election Of U.S. President, One Person = One Vote)

* Limit US Supreme Court Appointments to 6 years

* One House of Congress
(Sweden, Norway, Turkey, + Many More)

* Congress Selected Randomly
(Citizens Assembly, British Columbia, Canada)

* Recall of Congresspersons
(Articles of Confederation, USA 1776)

* United States Broadcasting Company
(BBC, CBC, Australian Broadcasting Company)

* United States National University
(Australia National University, Seoul National Univers

* Participatory Budgeting at the National Level *(Brazil, Argentina, England, Chicago, New York City + More)*

About the Authors

Ted Becker has led many lives: Class clown of his high school; sports editor of his college newspaper; consumer researcher for a large Madison Avenue advertising agency; member of the legal staff for the Attorney General of New Jersey; military intelligence; law school professor; oft-cited academic; mediator; online journal editor; author of 14 books on law, politics and political science.

Patricia Lantz is a former stylist and business owner, an Atlanta based counseling astrologer, writer and editor of astrology on AllThingsHealing.com, an online community dedicated to holistic and alternative healing of mind, body, spirit and planet.

Special Offer

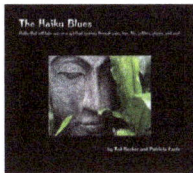

The Haiku Blues, Deluxe Limited Edition is in coffee book format, 13" x 11" and 170 pages, printed on highest quality photo paper. It's amazing to look at and at times seems like it's printed in 3D. This is not a book you will put on a shelf and forget. It's a book that will enhance your décor and that you'll want to be constantly within reach so you easily pick it up and meditate on some of your favorites. Given its size and dazzling quality, we are offering only 300 of our "Deluxe Limited Edition" at $295. Each book will be numbered and inscribed by the authors in any way you request (that's legal and doesn't violate The Patriot Act). If interested and want more details just email, becker.ted@gmail.com or write Dr. Ted Becker, 4707 Pebble Shore Drive, Opelika, AL 36804, for more details